What the World is About

How to Experience and Cope with the World

TOMAS K.

DEDICATION

This book is dedicated to all the Humans with the open mind and the peaceful heart.

CONTENTS

ACKNOWLEDGMENTS

I am very grateful to my wife Zuzana for her inspirational opinions
and thoughtful conversations that enriched this book.

Tomas K.

1 INTRODUCTION

It is my opinion, that our World appears to us as a fascinating miracle, invoking
>enchantment,
>fascination,
>humility,
>admiration,
>respect,
>sometimes fear.

We have a unique privilege
>to live in It
>to notice It
>to observe It
>to explore It
>to study It
>to think about It
>to gain insight in It
>to get knowledge about It
>to admire It
>to use It
>to enjoy It
>to be grateful for It
>to respect It.

Most probably, even You do like thinking about topics like:

Who am I?
>What is the life?
>Why do I live?
>How should I live?
>What is the purpose of my life?
>Who cares about me?
>Is there somebody or something who/what governs my life?

Is my life on the Earth just one episode of my lasting existence?

What is the World around me?
  Which parts and processes consist the World of?
  What is the structure of the World?
  How is the World organized?
  Who/what organizes the World?[1]

What is my position in the World?
  What is my role/task in the World?
  What opportunities/ways/styles/ are there in the World?
  How can I use them?
  What threats are there on the World?
  How can I cope with them?
  How should I cope with People/Society around me?
  How should I cope with Nature which surrounds me?

Why is the World as it is?
Why does the World exist?
….. and many other questions.

It is our great advantage, that generations of Humanity have gathered a huge amount of experience, ideas and knowledge on what, how, why, where, when, …. is going in our World. That is why we (I mean the contemporary and next generations of Humankind) can use them to answer, elucidate, evaluate, improve, extend, and precise the above introduced and other emerging issues.

In this my book, I will try to illustrate and offer my personal approach to the above-given topics. Maybe, they will inspire You and other people to improve and extend this (my) way of understanding of the World.

---

[1] *Note: The symbol „/ "is used in the text to express „and/or".*

2 WHO/WHAT AM I

I and You, we are human beings, which appeared in the materialized World - most probably - thanks to:

    ideas/desires/decisions/.... of my/your parents,

    natural processes of reproduction, which were made possible by existence, properties, and functions of:

        reproductive body organs of my/your parents,

        conditions for my/your proper prenatal development,

        birth, breastfeeding, parents´ caring about me/you

        upbringing me/you, ensuring material and other conditions for my/your life by my/your parents,

    gaining/deriving/gathering of my/your own experience and cognition of the people,

    processes and the World around me/you,

    learning, schooling, and education of the knowledge gathered by Mankind,

    my/your physical and mental development,

    my/your own everyday activities, gaining experience, skills, knowledge, material and other condition to survive and live my/your life.

We consist of our bodies, of our souls, minds, and of our experience, skills, and knowledge about the World around us. We have got/acquired/created the necessary material conditions, social and other relations to experience our lives among other people/Humankind, and to live in the World.

The World we live in is infinitely multiform in its parts, structures, processes, movements, transformations, changes, laws, intelligence, organization, mutual conditionality, mutual interactions, contingencies, etc.

Nevertheless, I espouse the idea, that the World is knowable/ recognizable/descript-able in its principles. I will illustrate this on several subjects/topics, starting with a description and an emplacement of myself (as a Human, one of the Humankind) in the World.

According to the standard biological organization scheme (*see: Bernstein R., Bernstein S., Biology, Wm. C., Brown Publishers, 1996. ISBN 0-697-15105-0.*), Humankind consists of groups of humans living together with populations of other living organisms in proximate physical (abiotic) environments creating specific ecosystems. All of the ecosystems make up the biosphere - the area of life on Earth.

The Biosphere, as well as all of its "components"/plants/ animals/humans/and others, follow their specific laws of nature encoded in their structures and functions, exist in their specific space/territories, in their specific time/lifetime regime(s), represent/need/generate specific energy or energy processes, they need resources/food/nourishment, watering/ drinking, light, heat, they exist in materialized/physical form(s) – in relation/connection/ interactions with parts, i.e. animals/plants/ humans/and others in the surrounding physical world, they take (actively or passively) specific stances/directions of action/directions of movement, i.e. they can move away in case of a danger or on the contrary approach pleasant sites, companies, etc. , they are acquired by a specific amount of information/intelligence to survive and develop in their proximate surroundings, they are - more or less - rationally organized/ structured, they are incidentally/casually/randomly or intentionally influenced by the other biosphere components, and by other tangible and/or intangible entities, like terrain, weather, fear, and others. I – as well as you and each of Humans - we are a part of the Biosphere, too.

We consist of our body, organ systems and their parts, of our soul, mind, conscious, experience, knowledge, abilities, desires, emotions, feelings, and other attributes.

Each of our body systems and organs (like skeletal system, muscular system, circulatory system, respiratory system, nervous system (brain, spinal cord, nerve sensory system (ear, eye)), digestive system, urinary system, reproductive system, endocrine system, integumentary system, immune system), can be decomposed to different tissues, which consist of cells, some of them with specific groups of organelles (which consist of molecular and other components (like liquids, compounds, elements/atoms, ions, etc.) and of their specific interactions, functions and processes).

Our cells and organelles are formed by multiple (bio) macromolecules and molecules. They are built of atoms of elements, which are – thanks to chemical bonds – grouped into the specific molecules and/or their conglomerates, and other components and compounds, which exert specific interactions, functions, and processes in our body.

Chemical properties of our atoms are influenced/determined/ originated by specifics of their compositions from subatomic particles, i.e. electrons, protons, and neutrons and by specifics of their mutual bonding forces and interactions.

Even the subatomic particles have their components, structures and complicated interactions, transformations, properties, etc.

At each level of the hierarchy, specific functions, which are necessary for the control of life, are managed specifically. For example, changes in chemical properties of atoms in consequence of an radioactive radiation can cause changes/complications on the molecular/ macromolecular level, and consequently, on organelle, cell, tissue, organs, and whole body levels. Fortunately, our body system is equipped with various self-restoring/self-healing immune intelligent mechanisms on hierarchic levels, which protects our lives against incidental/casual/random or intentional/harmful/ dangerous interactions, influences, and interventions.

The healthy development of our body is obviously significant for our mental part of our personality, because our body and its organs (especially brain) can be understood as an "antenna" or "emitting and receiving equipment" which mediates our communication and contact with "the Intelligence" and other parts of our World and other entities of the Objective Reality (see more details on this topic below).

However, me, you and other people, we consist of more than just body organs, cells, atoms, subatomic particles and interactions among them and outer World. We have also our dreams, wants, feelings, desires, … We have our mental life.

Let´s try to deliberate about it now.

3 MENTAL LIFE

Our physical body and its components are relatively easy observable/recognizable by our natural sensors/senses (eyesight, hearing, touch, smell, taste) and by many scientific methods and devices and by our practical experience. However, the mental parts of human personalities are hidden by uncertain, hardly cognizable/ measurable/repeatable/verifiable cognition, methods, ideas, presumptions, etc.

In my mind, the principal problem lies in an understanding and features of the entity/notion of the Soul. Because, - as well as like a wind - we can feel it but we cannot see it. I think it is a pleasant warm feeling of joy, happiness, love, enthusiasms, or sorrow, we sometimes experience, which reveal the existence of our Soul, too.

Generally, we admit/conjecture/agree that it is the Soul which makes the human body (and not just human bodies) alive.

I can imagine, that deeply in our prenatal existence, we acquire - besides the body dispositions encoded in DNA information - also mental capacity/ability/stamina/endurance/toughness/power/skills faculty/aptitudes/bents/talents from our parents and ancestors. That is why people exhibit different physical and mental health, and quality of life, though they live in the same family and social environment.

I am of opinion, the soul is manifesting itself like the "Inner Power", special "Life Energy", and "Life Software" or "Login for connection to a Universal Intellect" which starts and keeps "in operation" all the above described hierarchic unconscious functions in the (alive) human body, and as conscious/cognition/mental/ intellectual activities of Human. The healthy Soul has a profound significance for a healthy and happy life of a Human.

It is our neural system which brings a tremendous amount of information from the outer World via our senses/sensors into our brain, which is capable to use them for the ensuring/ establishing/adjusting the stable/appropriate/healthy unconscious functions of our body on the individual hierarchic body levels and among them. As well as, it enables to use the tremendous amount of useful information from the outer World in a human mind for thinking, assessment, evaluating, learning, creating new/own opinions/ideas/theories/ designs/plans, decision making, and other intellectual activities. Moreover, there are generated also numerous moral stances/attitudes/emotions/likes or dislikes/ positive or negative feelings/feelings of enjoyment/pleasure/ indulgence/relish/ satisfaction/ success/joy/ pleasure/delight/treat/ merriment/happiness/love/ or grief/ sorrow/distress/sadness/ woe/ bereavement/heartache/loneliness/pain/ seclusion/solitude, etc. in our mind and in our Soul.

4 WHY THE POSITIVE THINKING IS SO IMPORTANT

Thanks to the brain activities, a Human can get and gather/remember and re-use his own and others´ experience and knowledge during his life, as well as, share them with other living people or with descendants in future generations.

It is a great privilege for Humans that they developed, and thus, they can use numerous ways, methods, procedures, knowledge/know-how, tools, equipment, mechanisms, machines, techniques, technologies, plants, industry/agriculture/architecture/building industry/economy/management and other branches, which enriched their possibilities how to experience/enjoy/live ever fuller/richer/more interesting/safer/longer more satisfying lives.

Human is capable of intentionally/consciously control/manage/ establish/ adjust/choose many of the conditions for his life – like:

- where to live - in which place/country/continent/ climate/ society/….,

- with whom to live,

- to protect oneself against diseases, cold, heat, wind, floods, incidents with dangerous animals, plants, people, etc.,

- what to eat and drink,

- how to rest and sleep,

- what devote his lifetime to

    what to do useful and beneficial - for oneself, own family and others,

    which of his abilities he will develop/transform into useful purposeful works,

what leisure entertainment activities/ hobbies to practice,

what people/groups/companies/societies to meet,

which learning/ teaching activities.to develop,

- how to cope with unexpected situations,

- how to think and speak/communicate/report about himself and others,

- how to think and speak/communicate/report about the World around us,

- which knowledge/experience/advice/instruction coming from our surrounding World to admit/accept/respect or reject/refuse,

et cetera.

It is obvious that - as well as our body processes demand specific conditions, care, feeding, maintenance, etc., – even our mental processes demand their specific attention. Especially, the proper functions of the brain are dependent on appropriate surrounding conditions (like an access to quality air, temperature, (sun-)light, moisture, noise, etc.), proper nutrition and drinking regimes, a suitable/adequate load/employment, a profound sleep, rest and other conditions for its functions. Moreover, it needs also proper stimuli for its mental activities.

Our brain is ready to fulfill any of our conscious and/or unconscious will/desire/wants. That is why we should be aware, which of them, we generate in our mind intentionally/unintentionally/arbitrarily, are positive for us or - on the contrary - are harmful/detrimental/ derogative/ undesirable/unwholesome.

While thinking, speaking, writing, communicating ... about ours or others´ episodes, or while listening to anybody, to radio, watching on TV, reading books, etc., our brain can interpret some of the ideas/opinions/stances/situations, which attracted our attention, as an order to realize them, too, even if they would be detrimental for us.

That is why we should - time to time - consult/meditate with our mind and "Inner Power" what are our real wants and desires, and identify any false/undesirable ones and stop them. It makes a difference if our brain, mind, reason, mental capacity, soul, and also body processes are employed by new/original/personal/pleasant/ interesting/entertainment/useful/ enriching positive experience/ enjoyments rather than by dreadful/ senseless/worth-for-nothing ones.

As an example can be making a decision on preparation and realization of a private journey into a remote foreign country, which covers many financial, health protection, travel/accommodation/ nutrition/incentive program organization, travel clothing, shoes and other necessities preparation, notion of the local attractions, opportunities and threats, basics of local language, and many other relatively complex and demanding - but very exciting activities, full of positive expectations and enjoyment for ones who are internally motivated for such activities. But they could be a nightmare for somebody else who likes calm, safety, comfortable life.

However, creation of suchlike personal/original/own programs and of course also smaller ones (like planning and realizing family party, a one-day trip, visiting friends, an rearrangement of a terrace garden, creating a photo-book from the last trip, etc. are recommendable, even if they would demand rather more life/mental energy than a passive sitting and watching crime, war, problematic stories on TV or wasting a lot of time in "a blah blah chatting" parties.

I admit it demands some effort to avoid/stop thinking on negative aspects of own and other people behavior, society, politics, and others. However, it pays to practice the positive assessment of any situations and aspects of our and other people lives and to foster/promote and spread goodness everywhere and every time when possible.

I think it is very important for establishing the healthy and proper function of our inner homeostasis. Our brain, other parts of the nerves system, and other healing mechanisms will be unconsciously oriented to the proper "healing" processes on all the above mentioned hierarchical functional levels in our body. As well as, they will be consciously focused on meaningful/effective mental activities, on experiencing of our own life, positive emotions and on the feeling of own wellbeing.

It is very important, how and with what we "feed" our mind and our soul, and how we use and "satisfy" them.

5 WHAT IS OUR SURROUNDING WORLD

Our own senses (eye, hearing, touch, smell, taste), experience, cognition, everyday activities, as well as mediated knowledge, experience, results of everyday activities and of scientific and   philosophical research of Humankind, reveals that our World consists of individual/specific/separate entities/elements/parts/ components, which are in mutual interactions, which are governed by laws of nature.

According to my understanding, the origin and development, and the features of the World (which I understand as a part of the Objective Reality in the philosophical sense) can be explained/ described on the basis of the following axioms:

1.   There had existed four principal categories of the Objective Reality before our Universe/World came into its existence/appeared/ originated, i.e. in the "state" of singularity:

Laws of Nature (in the sense of "Lex Naturalis"),

The Potential of our "Real" World to exist (but not yet in an existence),

Contingency, and

Communications/relations/interactions.

2.   At the beginning of our Universe/World: the Potential for the existence of the Physical World started – contingently – its actualization/realization, respecting/by the Laws of Nature, and thus changed or transformed itself into Forces, which gave an origin to the Real Physical World, with its observable quantities (see

Note 1):

Time,

Space,

Energy,

Direction/Polarity,

Information,

Intellect,

Potential to exist,

Contingency.

They transformed themselves/give rise/developed/gave an origin to all observable individual elements, parts, processes, ... of the World (see below).

Note 1:

Why the Mass/Matter/Fields are omitted among the above observable quantities?

I came to the conclusion, that a mass/matter and fields could be understood as forms of an energy, which are specifically "structured", widespread and/or "locked in a space" under specific laws of nature. They can interact specifically with the other principal categories (i.e. space, time, direction, information, laws, intellect), appearing specific properties, and individual/specific elements, parts, processes, etc. of the Objective Reality (although hitherto unknown in all details).

This could acquire/give specific features to Mass/Matter objects, like: an inertia, gravitation, ability to change/modify fields, space-time structures and dimensions, particle structure, electric charges, electric, magnetic and electromagnetic properties and phenomena, attractive and repulsive forces, mechanical properties of matter, storing and conversions of energy, and phenomena which are intrinsic to all of the physical, inorganic, organic, living, thinking etc. objects and/or phenomena in the Nature and World.

14

The postulated "locked-space" principle of mass particles existence might elucidate naturally the observed deformation of a space-time structure around mass objects and the related phenomenon of gravitation, too.

It all might help to reveal further consequences to a better understanding of our World.

3.   These individual basic quantities are „present "/included or are „acting " in individual elements, parts, processes, ... of the Objective Reality as multiples of their elementary quanta (see *Note 2*).

Note 2

The following values of the basic elementary quanta are known for:

Time (Planck's Time): $5.39116(13) \times 10^{-44}$ *s,*

Space (Plank's Length): $1.616229(38) \times 10^{-35}$ *m*

Energy (Hartree): $4.359744650(54) \times 10^{-18}$ *J*

(see: CODATA, https://physics.nist.gov/cuu/Constants/index.html, August 7th, 2017.),

Others can be understood as follows:

Direction/Polarity: *+/-, or up/down, or forward/backward, etc., respectively;*

Information: *bit*

Intellect: *the individual/specific Laws of Nature inherent/obtained in the specific elements/processes of the Objective Reality;*

Potential to exist: *probability <0;1>*

Contingency: *arbitrary act in development of the World.*

4.   The individual basic quantities, elements, parts, processes, ... of the
Objective Reality exist in mutual interactions.

Note 3

*These interactions cause changes, transformations and/or motions/appearance or
disappearance of the individual basic quantities of Space, Time, Energy,
Direction/Polarity, Information, Intellect, Potential to exist, Contingency, and elements,
parts, processes, ... of the Objective Reality as a whole, respectively.*

*In other words, the elements, parts, processes, phenomena, etc. of the Objective Reality can
be expressed/composed/derived/ characterized by means of the above mentioned basic
quantities, as "a result" of all mutual interactions of existing elements and processes.*

(For better understanding - see below the description of the human body.)

5.   Transformations or motions of the elements, parts, processes, ... of
the Objective Reality are governed by „grammar ", or „syntax " rules,
which are usually known or understood as the Laws of Nature.

Note 4

*These rules are included in elements, parts, facts, features, attributes, ... of the Objective
Reality, too.*

*They are „applied", or "realized" via quantities of Information, Intellect, and
Direction/Polarity, i.e. they can be expressed by means of multiples the elementary quanta
of information, intellect, and direction/polarity.*

6.   The interactions among the elements, parts, processes, ... of the
Objective Reality can change sometimes just only some of the
characteristic dimensions, or values, or quantities, etc. of elements,
parts, processes, ... of the Objective Reality.

Note 5

That is why these interactions can repeatedly result in relatively stable forms of individual subjects (elements, parts, processes, ...) of the Objective Reality.

7. Actualization/Realization/Existence of the individual eventualities in the Objective Reality, including its state or form as a whole, is in principle contingent, even though some of their consequences may be relatively stable and repeatable as has been mentioned in paragraph 6 above.

Note 6

An occurrence/appearance/origin of our World and other entities and events on our Planet, or in our life can be results of the Contingency manifestation.

Remarks

Let me elucidate/explain/discuss now a few consequences/features included in this my stance:

This approach considers/states/underlines the significance of the laws of nature, intelligent/rational organization/ structuring/ functioning, as well as of the physical Quantities and other entities, and the Contingency for the origin and development of the World (as a part of the Objective Reality).

The above-mentioned Quantities and interactions could be denoted as our "World Existence Dimensions". In other words: our World consists of the components, such as:

a. The Laws of Nature (which we are trying to reveal/discover/describe/use...),

b. The Physical Entities/Quantities - Space, Time, Energy, Direction/Polarity, Information, (which we can observe, measure, study, use, to work with them, to modify them, ...),

c. The Potential to exist, to be actualized/realized

d. The Contingency,

e. The Intellect (which enables to learn, get and to structure knowledge, experience and information, intentionally use the Laws of Nature, and properties/ features of the physical entities, and also to estimate consequences of contingency variants/changes, ...), which are in a mutual interactions/ communications/ motions/ modifications.

According to this concept, the real specific processes, objects, entities, substances, phenomena, knowledge, etc. can be defined, described, "constructed", actualized, realized using multiples of the above given basic elementary quantities and their interactions. It respects the fact, that each of "proto-elementary" particles, each of photons and other suchlike entities do "know" how to behave, and what properties they "should hold" to become a part of a structure of large-scale particles, atoms, molecules, cosmic nebulas, and/or other structures, formations and bodies, including various other mutually interacting material bodies (elements), which result in an appearance and development of living self-reproducible forms of organisms, living nature, including human beings and society. (See *examples below.*)

It is a positivistic/scientific knowledge, which brings us to the conviction, that these properties and behavior – and thus the relevant natural laws, as well – have not been changed in the course of a whole development of the World since the Big Bang till now. That is the reason why we can – within certain limits - describe the evolution of the World in its principal features logically and persuasively, in accordance with an empirical observation and experimental verification testing, e.g. on the basis of positivistic knowledge and experience, and verified theories.

The aboriginal Potential to exist, the initializing Big Bang contingency, and the Laws of Nature, gave appearance/ origin to the Forces, which actualized the Potential - in accordance with Laws of Nature – gradually in the course of expanding Time and Space into[2]:

a. Intra-particle forces, which "stick together" particles and originate their characteristic properties, behavior and parameters, which enable us to recognize, define, denote, and classify them, respectively, as well as to generate them artificially, and to employ their properties intentionally in some cases and extent (like in colliders, nuclear power reactors, in medicine, and other applications).

b. Inter-particle forces and phenomena, which are denoted as nuclear forces and phenomena,

c. Atoms, isotopes, ions, atomic forces and phenomena.

d. Physical forces and phenomena, i.e. mechanical, gravitation, electric, magnetic, electromagnetic, etc. forces and phenomena.

e. Chemical forces and phenomena.

f. Molecules, radicals, molecular, as well as inter-molecular forces and phenomena.

g. Biological objects, forces and phenomena.

h. Human, human intellectual, psychological, and sociological forces and phenomena.

i. Humankind, community society, social and cultural forces and phenomena.

j. Political forces and phenomena.

k. Other objects, forces and phenomena.

---

[2] *Drawn up by myself using information from Wikipedia.*

The basic Quantities are "encoded"/or they evince/reveal themselves as attributes of physical objects, which are known (or were defined, or denoted, respectively) as fields, photons, sub-nuclear and nuclear particles and anti-particles, atoms, molecules, nebulas, suns, solid objects, asteroids, comets, planets, galaxies, and others.

The mentioned forces, phenomena, processes have been evolving gradually in the course of the expanding Time in specific locations of Space variously/heterogeneously, participating in the evolution of the World, Life, and Nature. They have been involving also in an origin and development of recurring natural forms and formations, living organisms, flora, fauna, including human beings and their society, etc. from the environment of the "natural" chaos. They are predominantly transitory, however, exhibiting some steady, consistent, firm, and suchlike forms just for relatively short or longer duration, only. (A s*hark is a shark with the same phylogenetic features for more than 400 million years.*)

During the origin processes, the principle of specific/recurring/dynamic balance of attractive and repulsive, and/or creative and destructive, emergence and annihilation etc. forces and other phenomena were acting.

It underlies the occurrence of particles, atoms, molecules, crystalline substances, physical objects, all natural products, planets, living organisms, and other forms of the known Universe.   In case that one or the other of the pole forces or phenomena prevail, destruction or transformation of specific forms and formations appear.

Thus, the real specific processes, objects, entities, substances, phenomena, knowledge, etc. can be defined, described, "constructed", actualized, realized on the basis/using the elementary quantities and their interactions.

The interactions between the individual elements, parts, processes, …. of the Objective Reality have been studied by special sciences - as a rule - under specific conditions, keeping (or reducing) some of the quantities constant or unchanged.

(For example, the interactions - according to specific rules (laws) - among the space, time, and direction quantities can give rise to/ describe such phenomena as velocity or acceleration.
The interaction between velocity and mass, according to the specific rule characterizes the phenomena known as a kinetic energy. Details of these and further interactions are studied by physics (mechanics).

The suggested concept enables to describe (or to express or to „absorb", etc.) all of the known quantities, characteristics, phenomena, elements, parts, processes, laws, behavior etc. of the Objective Reality on the basis of positivistic knowledge and experience and verified theories, because many of the discussed categories and phenomena have been yet studied, known, and applied in human practice relatively successfully.

This concept enables also to structure systematically - on the "sub-microscopic", „microscopic ", and/or „macroscopic " levels - all of the quantities, elements, parts, processes, ... of the Objective Reality, including the interactions, relations, laws, among them, even though they have not been known completely/ correctly/precisely, or at all so far. Thus, the concept can be helpful also in searching for such potentially existing, but so far omitted and unknown features of the Objective Reality.

It also describes the fact that the "individual cosmoses" are continually born and passed – in the frame of "our" current universe, e.g. at the genesis of a new human being, or a new knowledge, or of some artifact, and others.

The above-mentioned principles sum up the accessible knowledge of the World and its inherent laws and behavior, as well. They are in "natural" agreement with these laws and experience. They respect and absorb the basic cosmological findings, as well as the knowledge and experience, which have been gathered by special natural science, such as physics, logic, mathematics, chemistry, biology, etc.

Moreover, it provides also a sufficient "intellectual space´" to incorporate all the "superstructure" sciences and branches such as technology and engineering, informatics, cybernetics, as well as psychology, sociology, aesthetics, pedagogy, history, art and cultural sciences, theology, and others, into a homogeneous scientific environment.

The introduced theory does not solve the problem why the World emerged and why it has got just such parameters and behavior as it has/owns/exhibits. It is focused on the two principal questions: how the World was originated and how it has been developing so far and – probably how it will develop in the future.

These philosophical aspects may help us to improve and deepen our scientific knowledge, and also may enable solving some practical tasks - sociological, psychological, ecological, and others.

Hopefully, the critical verification of the suggested theory by individual scientific and branch specialists, philosophers and others, will make it more precise, comprehensive and applicable in further scientific, technical, social etc. branches.

I realize myself, that it is terrible to imagine that we – Humans - are ("just only") live entities, which – from the physical point of view – are the sophistically structured energy in a space and time, and which are endowed with an intellect, soul, mind/conscious//reason/ creativity, ideas, feelings, etc., and which are dependent prevailingly on own abilities and activities, and on random interactions with other entities of the World.

It is also difficult to accept the notion, that our body is not continuous/massive one, but it is prevailingly an empty and discontinuous space (*that is why it is transparent for X-ray and other short-wave electromagnetic irradiation*) and relatively tiny in comparison with the outer World dimensions.

The very significant might be the fact, that it is our soul, mind, and mental processes and activities, which can be connected to/can communicate with a longtime mental development (in past, now, and future) of the Humankind and to the Intelligence and processes/interactions/ parts/entities of the Objective Reality.

6 OUR ROLE IN THE WORLD

We should think/meditate/communicate/chat – separately/alone/ intimately – with our self/with our own Inner Power/our Soul at times, also about our role/impact in the outside World. As individuals, we can/we are capable - more or less - influence intentionally conditions and development in our proximate World, i.e. in our families, among friends, in workplaces, in neighborhoods, in local communities, in regional/state politics, economy, climate environment, etc.

The feeling of a considerate using of the resources, which we need for our life and activities, protective behavior to the flora and fauna, as well as the positive fair relations with people and a human society around us can be – in my mind – very important/strong impulses and resources for our mental and physical body health.

I am of an opinion, that a role/purpose of a Human is also to observe and reveal the essence/principles/laws of nature/ intelligence/parts/structure/ functions/processes etc. in the World.

People with strong/powerful/educated/cultivated mind/reason, who use their intellect to the searching and realizing ways how to live fully, in a good wellbeing, without harmful impacts for future life in the World, enjoy a very strong life satisfaction and appreciation of other mentally developed/ cultivated people and of themselves.

Searching laws of nature and formulating them for others, observing plants, animals, waters, minerals, hearing birds singing and other sounds in life nature, as well as music, arts, thinking about and doing goodness for our family members, friends, other people/community/country/World, and other mental activities can resonate with our mood/mind/reason/ understanding and an ability to accept/experience/hear/watch/notice the nice essence of notion, sounds/music, pictures/arts, colors, shapes, ... They can generate pleasant, healthy "celestial" feelings in our Soul. Thanks to the systematic learning and practicing the connection between our own Soul via nervous system/body parts with the outer World the feelings could be very strong and uplifting for us.

Vice versa, our happy Soul, enthusiastic/attentive/ conscious/ satisfied mind full of positive mental activities and attainable/ realistic meaningful intentions and plans, can result in better functions of the above mentioned hierarchical functional levels in our body, physical activities, and overall healthy body and spirit, better experiencing the World and our wellbeing.

It is obvious, that it is I/you/we, who is primarily responsible for own inner happiness, strong physical and mental health, wellbeing, and an acceptance by other people and a community. It is we who should care about ourselves using our Soul, mind, reason/brain, knowledge, experience, skills, and options existing in our surrounding World.

7 WHAT IS MY POSITION IN THE WORLD

My idea about my role and tasks on the World is based on the principles formulated above in the previous 6 Chapter "Our role in the World". Namely, on the fact, that I am lucky to use my conscious mind/reason/intelligence/body to control what/how I really want to do in my life, and to - more or less - influence some conditions and development in my proximate World, i.e. in my family, among my friends and my students, in neighborhood, in local community, in regional/state politics, economy, climate environment, etc.

I feel, that it is very important for my life satisfaction to use reasonably/responsibly the resources, like water, food staff, housing, clothing, which I need for my life and activities, and to enjoy, use and protect the flora and fauna, as well as positive fair relations with people and human society around me at my home country, and in the World while travelling into foreign countries.

I am of opinion, that my role/purpose as a Human is also to observe and reveal the essence/principles/laws of nature/intelligence/parts/ structure/ functions/processes etc. in the World. I am lucky that I could devote the considerable part of my life to intensive material science studies, to an execution of managerial duties, as well as to contemporary university activities, and thus to add something positive to the World.

There are many other opportunities/ways/styles in the World, which we can use, realize and develop. I think, everybody has the opportunity to "tailor" his personal content of life, which could be very different and original, in comparison with every other individuals´ one. For human society needs lots of very different professionals at disposal, like bakers, tailors, teachers, gardeners, laborers, farmers, medical doctors and nurses, train/bus/tram/car drivers, various employees and employers, actors, musicians, sportsmen, and thousands of other professions. Everybody can find his/her favorite position, which can contribute to/create his/her full satisfaction with her/his purpose in life, and hence to his/her mental and overall health.

However, besides fulfillment of duties, there are also opportunities for free and leisure time activities and experiences in the World, which make us satisfied and happy. Everybody can choose nowadays – even being handicapped – his/her satisfying hobby/hobbies, practicing actively or passively like: reading, writing, learning/teaching, studying, communicating, public speaking, singing, playing musical instruments, dancing, dramatic arts, fine arts, sports, travelling, hiking, camping, gardening, and thousands of other activities or just resting, relaxing, meditating, enjoying chatting, thinking, etc. They can boost, fulfill and enrich our experience, feelings, notion, minds, and Souls, i.e. mental lives, but also they can balance and improve our physical body processes and overall health.

It is our Inner Power/mind/reason/intelligence that leads us to the decision/motivation/ determination, which of the opportunities we really want to use and actualize/realize/enjoy in our life. It´s prevailingly just we, who can make us happy and satisfied with our lives and deeds.

Of course, there are also threats and risks in the World, which can threaten our health, existence, and life. They can come from the outer World, like earthquakes and volcanic activities, storms, floods, droughts, extreme frosts or heats, diseases, epidemics, famines, accidents, crime, riots, wars, etc.

Some of the human handicaps can be inherited/congenital. They can cause some limits in the broadest palette of opportunities for our life. However, on the other hand, they can lead/focus us to something special, deeper, and valuable in the World, which can fulfill our life with impressive works, rich experience and happiness, too.

Lots of threats come from our own decisions, and activities. They come from/can be related to our lower ability/will to think thoroughly about our own life purpose/wants/goals and ways/plans/measures/moves how to focus on to realize, experience and enjoy them in fulfilled happy life.

Sometimes, it is seemingly easier to follow examples/advice/ instructions/orders on how to live, coming from our parents, family members, mates, friends, authorities and institutions, or literature/theatre/movie/TV authors, actors, characters and heroes, or successful sportsmen, pop-stars, writers, composers, inventors, scientists, V.I.P., and others. But, we can expect, that we can find/realize at the end of our life, that we lived/enjoyed/ experienced somebody else´s life conceptions, intentions, and dreams.

I personally vote for conscious, soul/mind/heart open-style of experiencing/enjoying living in our wonderful World. It is a matter of fact, that there are lots of threats and risks around us. However, we can identify/recognize/evaluate and avoid/reduce them in time, using either our own reason/brain, experience, knowledge, and skills, or using others´ stories, examples, advice, knowledge, instructions, expertize, errors and mistakes.

We can manage many of the risks and their consequences using modern health protective equipment (dressing, footwear, glasses, helmets, breathing apparatus, ropes, and many others) and regimes (nourishing, drinking, sleeping, resting, hygienic, …), employing modern advanced medical and healthcare methods, diagnostic, surgery and other devices/tools/ procedures/medications/ materials, etc., as well as modern communication and transport technologies, and techniques, emergency, safety and self-rescue advice/instructions, self-rescue procedures, etc.

Some annoying unpleasant mental and social limits and risks can be managed using traditional and modern soul/mental-healing procedures, like meditations, practicing yoga, regular physical exercising, relaxation massaging, etc. I personally recommend applying at times principles of neuro-linguistic programming (*See: Richard Bandler´s and John Grinder´s works*) and similar procedures, which are effective in a "cleaning and clearing up" of our mind and soul and in a setting/focusing them on our desirable/wanted topics and life programs, and on their actualization and enjoyment.

It sometimes demands an effort and/or outer assistance/support/ help of another person(s) to overcome/get rid of our own prejudices/ ideas/opinions/mental blocks and to cope with yourself, with people and society around us. Some people suffer from anxiety/feeling/effort to be the best/first/winner/perfect. However, there has been hardly one perfect Human living on the Earth.

It is great, that we have always a chance to be better/smarter/ beautiful/handsome/cleverer, more successful/more educated/influential/powerful …., if we want to. But it is strongly recommendable to appreciate/esteem/regard/accept/comprehend/perceive/see all of our own features as unique/personal/characteristic/identical/typical ones for us, and take/like/love the one we are.

I think, this attitude is very important for our open/free/unblocked/ intensive reception of other people´s opinions/wisdom/notion/ experience/significance, as well as for our unbiased/impartial/ unprejudiced stance and evaluation of achievements of the human society. In my view, those are principal keys, which enable us to "login to" and use the Intelligence encoded in people, human society, in the World Wide Web, and in the "Universal Wide Intelligence", which is a part of the elements/parts/ processes/ structures/organization and other phenomena in the World and in the Universe.

The openness in accepting/absorbing the tremendous wisdom/ experience/knowledge can give us the opportunity to use and enjoy lots of wonderful parts, facts, and phenomena of the surrounding Nature and cope with them.

I - and hopefully you, too - always feel an amazing/astonishing/ fascinating respect and gratitude while observing and realizing the existence of stars, sun, dawn, sun rise, sun set, nightfall, moon, blue sky, clouds, water waves, drops in the rain, stream in a brook, in a river, life in a sea, in an ocean, glass of drinking water, wind in its various nuances, storms, lightning, volcanos, mountains, valleys, escarpments, hills, desert plateaus, rocks, minerals, crystals, stones, pebbles, sand, dunes, fertile soil, fields, meadows, pastures, grass, moss, lichen, mushrooms, cacti, succulents, water plants, shrubs, bushes, trees, woods, virgin and rain forests, jungles, parks, gardens, flowers, strawberries, blueberries, raspberries, currants, fruit bushes and trees, herbs, potatoes, grain, rice, carrot, parcel, celery, paprika, pepper, cabbage, cauliflower, zucchini, eggplant, cucumbers, etc., animals, like: ants, beetles, warms, moles, acres, mice, flies, butterflies, bees, bumble bees, wasps, hornets, horseflies, dragonflies, birds, hens, duck, gees, turkeys, guinea fowl, pigeons, snakes, amphibians, fish, crawfish, crabs, oysters, whales, many other mammals, like domesticated and utility animals - dogs, cats, goats, sheep, cows, pigs, horses, ox, mules, camels, wild animals – elephants, rhinoceros, hippos, buffalos, lions, leopards, cheetahs, giraffes, zebras, antelopes, kudus, jackals, hyenas, baboons, and other animals living in Africa, tigers, orangutans, and other living in Asia, kangaroos in Australia, deer, hares, foxes, badgers, wild boars, fallow deer, living in my country. Of course, this enumeration represents only the tiny part of my experiences that accidentally emerged in my mind when writing this text.

I am also fascinated by what achievements Humanity has reached in learning the world and in endeavoring to facilitate and improve the safety of life on Earth. There have been created/invented/ developed amazing tools, aids, mechanisms, machines, devices, equipment, ways of production, technologies, new materials, chemical staffs, health and medical care procedures, medicines, foodstuffs, etc., thanks to the human ability to pass/communicate/enrich/transfer the acquired experience, knowledge, skills and wisdom from generation to next generation.

The remarkable feature of people is their ability to create their own ideas about the World and to develop them into philosophical/scientific/artistic pictures/expressions/descriptions/displays, which are understandable/ intelligible/graspable/digestible by their conscious minds, and Souls.

Especially, I am curious about the human ability to transfer/communicate feelings – like a joy/happiness/sadness/likes/dislikes/enthusiasms/ disappointments/fears/hopes/expectations/enjoyments, etc. experienced/ gained/acquired during human lifetime – to others via music, visual arts, dramatic arts, and other works and media.

Of course, I realize myself, that the above enumeration of the remarkable facts, processes, features, experiences, … that our World offers us is far from complete. I wanted just to come to conclusion, that these and others items reflect themselves in our lives, and that we are influenced/co-created by the status/results/facts and by of longtime historical development of all the details in our World.

8 EPILOG: HOW TO COPE WITH THE WORLD

I have formulated many suggestive questions in the Introduction. I have given answers to some of them in the previous text. Nevertheless, I will try now to summarize/formulate/add some further (my own/subjective) opinions/notion on all of them in the "Q&A" form, as follows:

Q: Who am I?

A: The answer to this question is given in the Chapter. "What/What am I?". I just add, that I am a lucky and happy Human fully experiencing and enjoying the miracles and beauties of the life in the World right now (on August 11th, 2017) and that I can leave a message about myself to other contemporaries and to people in future generations.

Q: What is the life?

A: It is a noble, valuable, precious, rare, uncommon, wonderful, splendid, terrific, stupendous, prodigious, glorious, admirable, bewildering, mysterious, sacred, fancy phenomenon, that we can experience and enjoy in the World.

Q: Why do I live?

A: The answer to this question is given in the Chapter "What/What am I?".

I add to it: I think, ….because of the many lucky/contingent/objective circumstances and conditions which have been realizing for many years in my closest neighborhood/proximate surroundings and in outer World, and because of my personal attitude/approach to the Life.

Q: How should I live?

A: The answer to this question is partly given in the Chapter "What/What am I?".

I just add: I am trying to live in harmony with natural and social laws, with common sense, respecting Life and Nature, respecting Human interests, and experiencing the opportunities for my life in the World.

Q: What is the purpose of my life?

A: The answer to this question is in part given in the Chapter "Our role in the World".

I only add I feel that the purpose of my own/personal life is to create conditions for the successful/healthy development of my own family and to add some useful insight and experience to support the sustainable development of the Humankind in the World.

Q: Who cares about me?

A: It is - first of all - me myself. Frankly said I cannot imagine my life without my wonderful wife and without her everyday lovely care about me.

My life is also dependent on the tremendous number of people in the frame/sense of the general "division of labor."

From the broader perspective, it can be anybody else who is interested in me, whose interests/lives would be affected by my existence/behavior/acts/works etc.

Q: Is there somebody or something who/what governs my life?

A: I think, yes. Above all, they are the Laws of Nature and the other above mentioned "World Existence Dimensions" or categories of the Objective Reality and interactions which govern my life, objectively.

Subjectively, my life is governed by the ethical rules, the legal system, social habits and norms, family rituals, etc. in my proximate living surrounding.

Q: Is my life on the Earth just one episode of my lasting existence?

A: I would be happy if at least some of my modest findings and results of my life activities/works/opinions last longer than my temporary life on the Earth.

What is the World around me?

Q: Which parts and processes consists the World of?

Q: What is the structure of the World?

Q: How is the World organized?

A: I hope, my answers to these questions were appropriately given in the Chapter "What is our surrounding World?"

Q: Who/what organizes the World?

A: I feel, the World is organized by the Laws of Nature, intelligently/ rationally in responses/relations to accidental/random/ adventitious/ contingent interactions and situations which have been happening all the time since the Big Bang.

Q: What is my position in the World?

Q: What is my role/task on the World?

Q: What opportunities/ways/styles/ are there in the World?

Q: How can I use them?

Q: What threats are there on the World?

Q: How can I manage them?

Q: How should I cope with People/Society around me?

Q: How should I cope with Nature which surrounds me?

A: I gave my explanation/opinions to the individual questions in the Chapter "What is my position in the World?"

Q: Why is the World as it is?

A: I think, this typical question of metaphysics could be answered – from the positivistic position - like: because it is in line/a consequence/feature/property/manifestation of the Nature/ Intelligence, and Laws of Nature, "World Existence Dimensions", elements, parts, interactions, other Categories and Principles of Nature.

I agree it is hard to imagine that the flowers/animals/people/…. goodness/badness …. have been created by the same Principles of Nature and that they were created by chance, on the basis of rules, principles without any aesthetic feelings, reason, intentions …

Fortunately, we – people - use our fantasy/feelings/imagination/ experience/reason/mind/Soul to answer the questions for ourselves in a more humanistic style. Thus, we have created our superstitions, hearsay, myths, religions, arts, literature, dramatic theatre, virtual reality… science, theories, …. everyday experience and activities, etc., which makes our reality more explainable, tolerant and pleasant; unfortunately, they are sometimes misused by too big ambitions/bad/dangerous people/authorities/rulers/ institutions/ organizations, …. against the other people.

Q: Why does the World exist?

A: Frankly/objectively said: No Human knows!

Even though there are many people/institutions/organizations/….., which declare, that they know the answer to this and suchlike metaphysical topics, and that is why they are approved to govern the other trustful people."

….. and many other questions.

Dear Readers,

please, specify some of the questions and send them to me: t.kala@centrum.cz. I will try to answer them all.

Sincerely Yours,

Tomas K.

9 INSTEAD OF CONCLUSIONS

Let´s be Humans with opened conscious Minds and Souls, who appreciate and enjoy theirs and others lives, and all the phenomena in the World!

You can think about the following messages, too:

I am a miraculous creature living in the World with you, too.

I am pretty well structured and full of Laws of Nature/Intelligence.

…….… and what about me and my child?

ABOUT THE AUTHOR

Tomas K. designed and published the Unitary Theory of the World, in 2008 (ISBN: 978-1-4251-7553-5). The revised version of the Theory and several related essays are available on his websites http://www.tomas-kala.net/products/revision-of-the-unitary-theory-of-the-world-2-/.

He studied chemistry, worked in material science (published about 15 papers, reached a DrSc degree), in managerial positions, and later on in management research and education (published more than 20 and articles and books, reached a DBA degree). Currently, he is working independently for the University of Hradec Kralove in the Czech Republic.